Mindful
Coloring Book for Adults

Stress Relieving Designs for Adults Relaxation, Meditation and Mindfulness

Copyright © 2019 Jeff Cooper
ISBN: 9781703088540

adult coloring relieving designs
coloring pencils designs relieving
coloring books for adults relaxation pencils
anxiety coloring books for adults

Love
Love

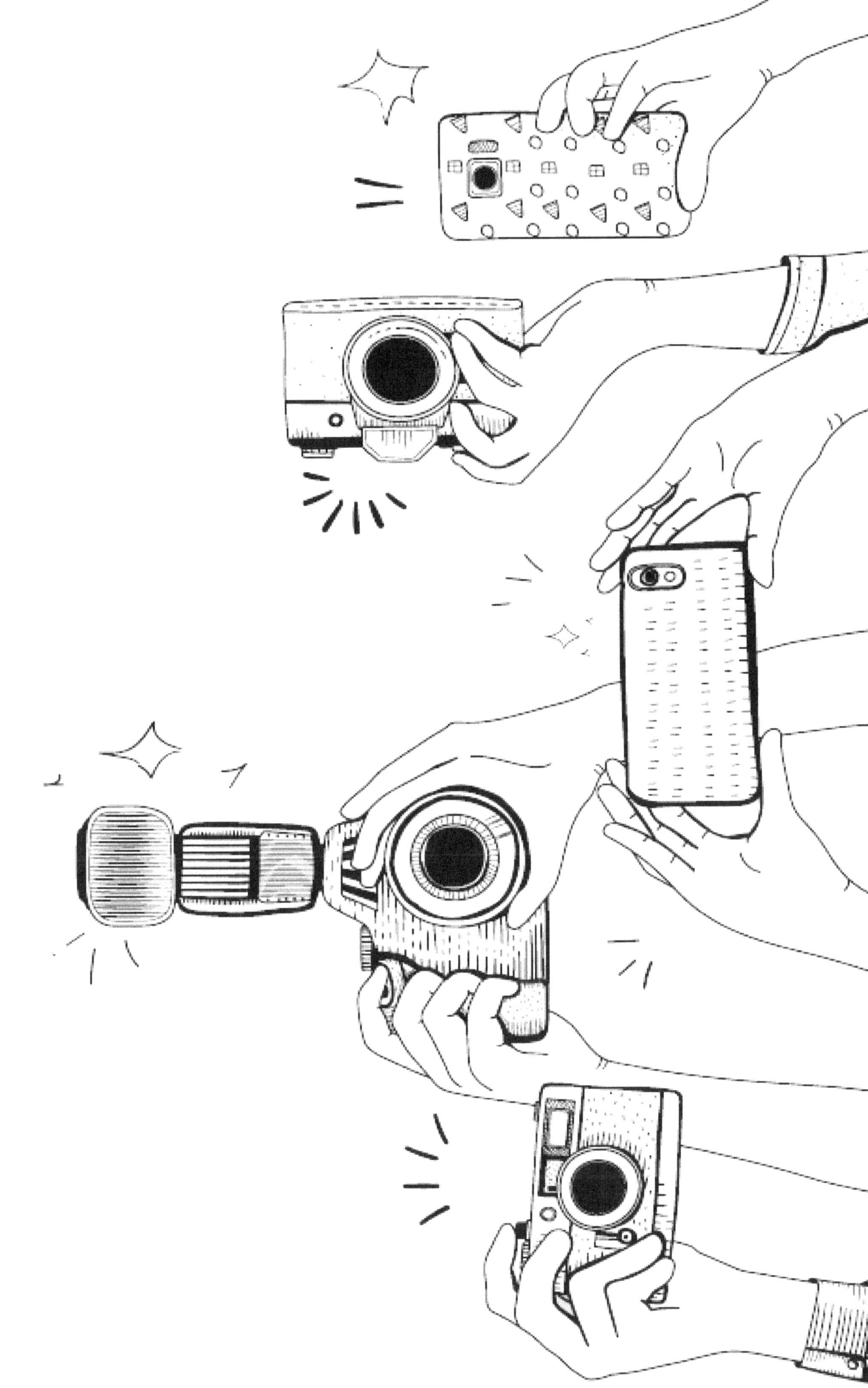

I ♥
Paris

TEA

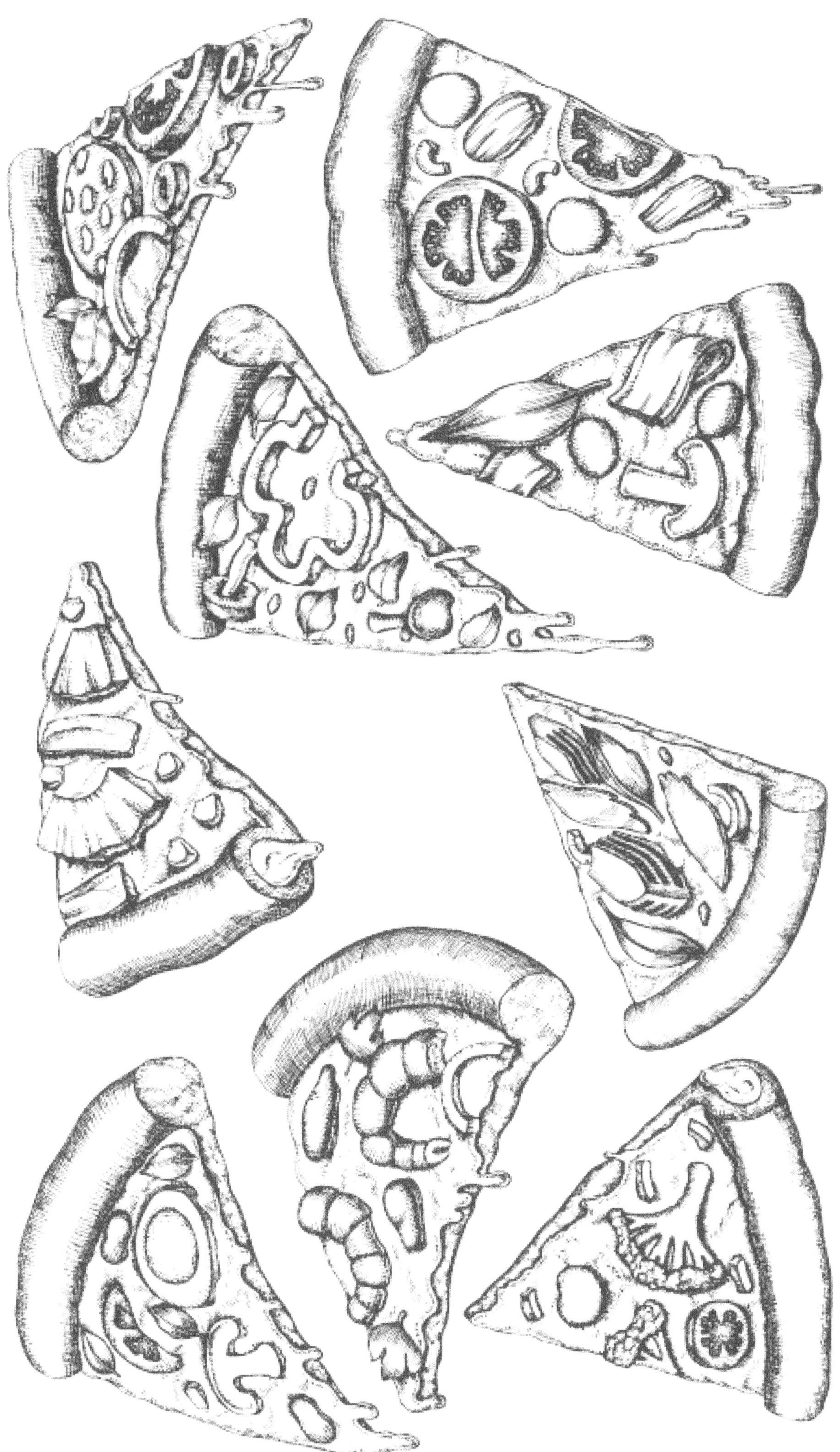

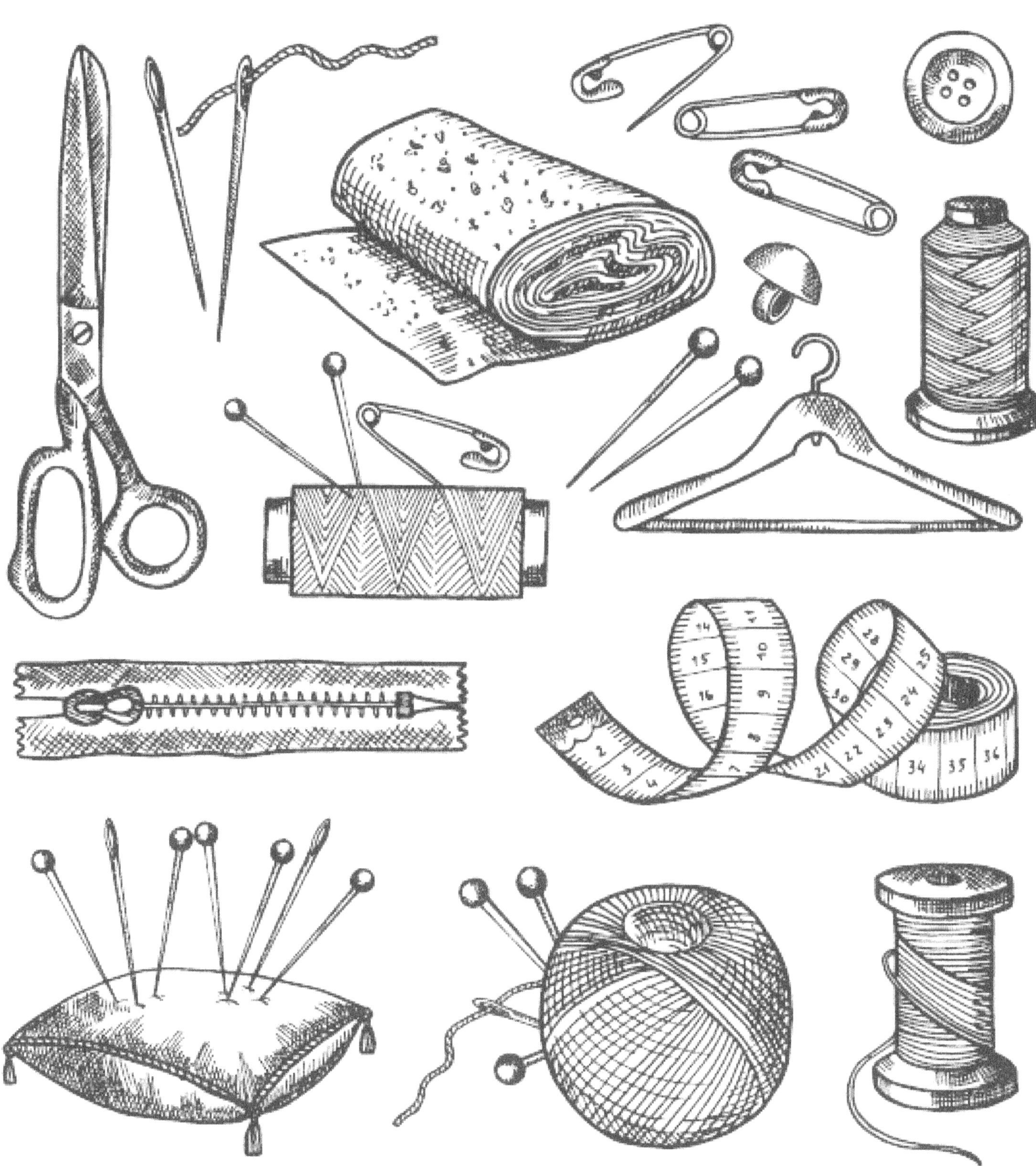

Test Color

Test Color

Test Color

www.ingramcontent.com/pod-product-compliance
Lightning Source LLC
Chambersburg PA
CBHW081727250726
48657CB00010B/3159